Sociology Revision
AS-Level
Education Revision &
Test Yourself Booklet
Ideal for Resits

SOCIOLOGYTWYNHAM.COM

ISBN-13: 978-1507859421
ISBN ISBN-10: 1507859422

ACKNOWLEDGEMENT

Special thanks to pixabay.com for allowing the use of their image on the front cover.

CONTENTS

PLEASE NOTE

This test yourself booklet has been designed to test your knowledge in the multiple-choice questions and understanding in the short question section.
First and foremost this is a revision guide book designed to supplement rather than replace your text book.
The guide has also been designed to accompany this booklet so you can address and misunderstandings you might have and improve your examination performance.

1 EDUCATION

SCHOOL SYSTEM AND TYPES OF SCHOOLS

In the same way politicians sought to promote certain types of family structures, they have and continue to influence the types of school there are in England and Wales through their social policies.

1944 Education Act – established 3 types of schools known as the tripartite system – grammar; technical and secondary modern schools. A process of selection via 11+ test determined which school you went to. The top 15-20% of those passing the 11+ went to grammar schools

Criticisms of tripartite system:

- 11+ was unreliable;

- the selection process was unfair and wasteful;

- cemented social-class divisions

Comprehensive Schools – unlike the tripartite system there is no selection test for entry to comprehensive schools. The development of comprehensive schools came in the 1960s as a reaction against tripartite system (but process of selection still occurs in some areas of England).

Comprehensives sought to:

- reduce social class divisions;

- break down social-class barriers

Conservative education policy (1979 – 1997)

- New Vocationalism 1986 (NVQs etc);

- The 1988 Education Reform Act introduced competition between schools and turned parents into 'consumers' of education. This process is often termed the marketization (free market) of education. New Right thinkers argue social policies are more effective if they are driven by free market principles. These principles are evident in the 1988 Education Act because the act introduced (in no particular order):

1. The National Curriculum
2. National testing (SATS)
3. National league tables
4. Open enrolment and parental choice
5. Ofsted
6. Local management of schools

New Labour's educational policy 1997 – 2010

- Specialist schools;
- Expansion of league tables (vocational GCSEs added as well as Contextual Value Added Scores);
- Equality of opportunity e.g. EMA; Education Action Zones (known as compensatory education)- page 23
- Expansion of numbers in FE and HE;
- Expansion of vocational education

Conservatives 2010 onwards

- Academies Bill;
- Free Schools:
- Bursary Scheme (replaced EMA);
- Vocational GCSEs axed from league tables;
- Changes to A-levels and GCSES
- Since 2010 there is now an even wider range of schools children can attend: Free schools, traditional Academies and Academy Converters all have the same status in law.

Independent Schools otherwise known as fee-paying schools are independent of government control.

COMPETING PERSPECTIVES OF EDUCATION

Functionalist perspective of education - Emile Durkheim – writing over 100 years ago, argued one of the main functions of education is to bind members of society together – this creates social unity and social solidarity. Therefore like the family, education is seen as a functional prerequisite because it helps pass on society's core values such as the division of labour.

Talcott Parsons writing in the 1950s developed Durkheim's ideas. He identified socialization (secondary) and social integration as two key functions of education, along with role allocation. Like Davis and Moore, Parsons' argued the education system functions to put the right people in the right jobs through a meritocratic system of role allocation.

For functionalists the key functions (purpose) of the education system are:

1. passes on society's culture – education helps establish a value consensus through the hidden curriculum (the hidden curriculum – how students learn behaviours, values, beliefs, and attitudes)
2. socialization - Parsons argues how schools take over the role of parents as sites of secondary socialization.
3. provides a bridge between particularistic values and universalistic values – schooling equips individuals with achieved status rather than ascribed status
4. provides a trained and qualified labour force – schooling equips people in society with the right skills needed to do their jobs creating a division of labour
5. meritocracy - Davis and Moore said the education system becomes the best mechanism for rewarding individual effort legitimising social inequalities

Marxist perspective of education - Louis Althusser (1971) argued that the main role of education in a capitalist society is the reproduction of an efficient and obedient work force. The working-class are 'accept' their exploitation by the ruling-class through several ideological state apparatuses such as the family and the education system. The education system is a particularly powerful ideological state apparatus because:

1. reinforces the ideology that capitalism is just and reasonable (schools teach pupils competition between each other is normal)

2. education system trains future workers to become submissive to authority (schools teaches pupils to accept being told what to do as normal, that way, when your boss orders you what to do, it seems perfectly normal)

Bowles and Gintis' study 'Schooling in Capitalist America' (1976) supported Althusser's ideas that there is a close correspondence (relationship) 'the correspondence principle' between the social relationships in the classroom and those in the workplace through:

1. the correspondence principle – schools processes are very similar to offices and factories, creating a long shadow of work through a system of top-down control and a hidden curriculum encouraging conformity

2. myth of meritocracy - schools legitimate the myth that everyone has an equal chance; so pupils think those people in the top jobs got there on merit when in fact those at the top are there due to their social-class background. In this way social inequality is legitimized and justified as natural

3. hidden curriculum – the school processes mentioned above which prepare students for workplace (rather than scholastic achievement) are reinforced through having to follow a timetable; being punctual; wearing a uniform; doing homework, are all part of the hidden curriculum (the 'visible' curriculum is your lessons, school assemblies, etc).

Bourdieu also sees the education system as reproducing and legitimizing social inequalities through his concept of social capital in order to explain how the middle-classes succeed while the working-class are less likely to (see page 22).

Paul Willis also adopts a Marxist approach when he studied the relationship between the education system and the workplace. His interactionist approach looked at working-class subcultural resistance (counter-culture) to the education system (see page 23).

Both functionalists and Marxists refer to the hidden curriculum. However they have distinct differences:

Functionalism and the hidden curriculum (positive)	Marxism and the hidden curriculum (negative)
1. pupils to look smart via the school uniform 2. punctuality through disciplining people who are late 3. shows children how to follow instructions 4. how to read and follow a timetable 5. teaches meritocracy - the benefits of working hard and doing additional work at home (homework)	1. school rules, detentions & rewards, teach people to conform whether you like it or not! 2. school assemblies teach respect for dominant ideas 3. boys and girls to accept different roles in society with boys learning to be masculine and girls feminine 4. to follow teachers' instructions without question in the same way you have to follow a bosses orders 5. being punctual, as your time belongs to your teacher/school and not you. This again replicates the way a future boss owns your time and so you're being prepared for the world of work!

Both functionalist and Marxist perspectives have other similarities:

- They are both structuralist approaches

- They both tend to ignore social processes within school (factors inside school) – except Willis

- They both tend to ignore the effect of the hidden curriculum on gender stereotyping

Despite their similarities functionalist and Marxist perspectives have their problems:

Problems with functionalism	Problems with Marxism
1. Differences in achievement in terms of gender, ethnicity and class questions the notion of a meritocratic education system 2. Education does not prepare students for the workplace as employers are often critical of the education system 3. It does not adequately explain how education serves the interests of certain groups through promoting certain values and ideologies	1. It assumes pupils are passive victims in the classroom – a point raised by Paul Willis 2. Most people see the inequalities in the education system and some parents challenge it by paying for their child's education 3. Some students work hard to overcome the inherent inequalities in the education system

Feminist perspective of education - for feminists the education system reinforces the social inequalities between the genders. This is achieved through:

1. gendered language – reflecting wider society, school textbooks (and teachers) tend to use gendered language – 'he', 'him', 'his' etc making women invisible
2. gendered roles – school textbooks have tended to present males and females in traditional gender roles – for example, women as mothers and housewives
3. gender stereotypes – reading schemes have also tended to present traditional gender stereotypes e.g 'boys are presented as more adventurous than girls'
4. women in the curriculum – in terms of what's taught in schools – the curriculum – women tend to be missing, in the background, or in second place and so 'hidden' from the curriculum mirroring society
5. subject choice – traditionally certain subjects were often seen as 'boys' subjects' and 'girls' subjects

Feminist perspectives have been valuable for exposing gender inequality in education. Partly as a result of sociological research, a lot has changed – for example, much of the sexism in reading schemes has now disappeared. Today, women have overtaken men on most measures of educational attainment.

FACTORS INSIDE SCHOOL AND FACTORS OUTSIDE SCHOOL AFFECTING ACHIEVEMENT

Despite numerous forms of social policy interventions by the state, significant class differences in educational achievement continue. Some sociologists focus on factors outside school as the primary cause for social class differences in educational achievement while others focus on factors inside school.

FACTORS OUTSIDE SCHOOL (material, cultural, linguistic deprivation and subcultural explanations)

Material deprivation

- Douglas' (1964) research identified material factors as the cause of working-class underachievement in schools. Material factors include, poor housing, poor diet etc. Gibson and Asthana (1999) found the greater the level of family disadvantage the smaller the percentage of students gaining 5 or more GCSE grades A* - C.

- A more recent piece of research by Lisa Harker (2006) also found a relationship between poor-quality housing and low attainment at school. Harker's research found:

1. less space to play, restricted a child's cognitive development
2. there was less space to study
3. increased likelihood of being bullied at school which increased truancy rates
4. higher stress levels of the parents, leading to less support

- Martha Farah (2006) researched the impact of socio-economic status on cognitive development and found that poverty had a direct impact on the development of a child's brain which ultimately affected their attainment at school.

- Furthermore the Sutton Trust (2005) found a direct relationship between free school meals and attainment. Top performing state schools had around 3% of their intake eligible for free school meals, whereas the majority of state schools had 14.5% of their intake eligible for free school meals.

Cultural deprivation

- Douglas also found cultural factors played an important part in a child's attainment at school. Douglas found middle-class parents compared to working-class parents:

1. took greater the parental interest in a child's education the greater the educational success
2. were better educated themselves and so better understood education system
3. more confident in dealing with schools/teachers
4. better able to help their child with school work

Cultural Capital

Bourdieu uses the term habitus to describe the cultural characteristics and values of each social-class. His point is middle-class children tend to thrive in school, as the culture of schooling is one which engages with cultural capital because:

1. cultural capital – the knowledge, language and values which readily translate into educational capital

2. upper and middle-class children succeed in school as they have more cultural capital

3. working-class children tend to lack cultural capital and so are more likely to fail in an educations system which 'enjoys' cultural capital

4. Bourdieu's point is that school looks like it is culturally neutral when it is biased towards the upper and middle-classes

Subcultural explanations

- Cultural differences are extended further by examining sub-cultural differences between social groups. Sugarman (1970) and Hyman (1967) highlighted the effects of socialization:

    1. Middle-classes socialised their children to – focus on future time orientation and deferred gratification facilitated by individual effort
    2. Working-classes socialised their children to – focus on present time orientation and immediate gratification due to a sense of fatalism

Linguistic deprivation – language and education

- Educational success is heavily dependent on language. Bernstein (1971) distinguished between restricted speech codes (can be used by both social classes but mainly lower working classes) and elaborated speech codes (used by middle-classes).

Compensatory education (positive discrimination) is used by the state to compensate for the social inequalities identified above affecting educational outcomes. Examples are:

1. Operation Head Start;
2. Educational Action Zones;
3. Educational Priority Areas;
4. Pupil Premium; 16 – 19 Bursary Fund

Factors Inside School (interactionist perspective) school organization, teacher interaction and pupil subcultures

The interactionist perspective does not see pupils as passive 'victims'- of material or cultural forces but as active in their relationships with teachers and their schools e.g. school council influencing the meaning they give to a situation.

School organisation

- Keddie (1971) challenges the notion of cultural deprivation, discussed above, as the root cause of educational failure. Instead Keddie shines the spotlight on schools themselves as failing to meet the needs of cultural diversity.

- Rutter (1979) also places a greater emphasis on schools themselves. The better their organizational structures and polices the better the school; policies such as: (listed overleaf)

1. homework policy
2. marking policy
3. teacher reward systems
4. mixed ability classes
5. teacher lesson preparedness

Teacher interaction

- Becker's research found teachers had a stereotypical image of an ideal pupil based on middle-class qualities, labelling the ideal pupil as bright and successful, the halo-effect. In contrast teachers stereotyped working-class pupils as lacking motivation and difficult to manage therefore are negatively labelled as thick or slow.

- Rosenthal and Jacobson (1968) research found positive and negative labels helped produce a self-fulfilling prophecy in the classroom, highlighting the value of an interactionist approach as pupils clearly 'active' in their relationships with teachers.

- Ball's study of Beachside Comprehensive examined the effect of banding and streaming on pupil performance. Ball found top stream students were warmed up while lower streamed/banded pupils were cooled down. Streaming of banding is often linked to social class – the higher your social class the higher the likelihood of being in a top stream/band.

    1. setting is where pupils of similar ability are put in different groups/sets in specific subjects
    2. streaming/banding involves grouping students of similar ability for every subject studied.

PUPIL SUBCULTURES

Male anti-school subcultures

- Hargreaves (1967) related the emergence of pupil subcultures to labelling and streaming. Colin Lacey's (1970) study of Hightown Grammar school also showed how streaming can lead to the creation of anti-school subcultures. Paul Willis (1997) in 'Learning to Labour' examined the effects of being placed in lower bands/streams. Though Willis adopted a Marxist approach he drew much from the interactionist perspective to compensate for the failings of the traditional Marxist model. Willis found working-class pupils rebelled against their being labelled as failures by acting the fool in lessons in order to enhance their status/self-esteem in ways other than academic ones.

Mac an Ghaill (1994) identified 3 working-class male subcultures

1. Macho Lads;

2. Academic Achievers

3. New Enterprisers

Female subcultures

- Scott Davis (1995) found girls' resistance to school was evident but less aggressive than their male counterparts due to their preoccupation with 'romance' and any future domestic roles. Abrahams (1995) identified female resistance to school as one based on pushing school rules to the limit. While Osler and Vincent (2003) suggest that girls are more likely to develop patterns of non-attendance when facing difficulties in school

- Margret Fuller (1984) found African Caribbean girls formed positive subcultures by working extra hard, determined to succeed despite experiencing racism in schools. In contrast C. Jackson (2006) 'Lads and Ladettes in School: Gender and the Fear of Failure' looked at how girls are forming anti-school subcultures and becoming ladettes because of the fear of academic failure.

African-Caribbean male subcultures

- Gaine and George (1999) found African-Caribbean subcultures develop from both factors inside and outside school.

African-Caribbean female subcultures

- Mac an Ghail (1998) found in general African –Caribbean girls are pro-education and ambitious. Margret Fuller (1984) found African Caribbean girls formed positive subcultures by working extra hard, determined to succeed despite experiencing racism in schools

GENDER DIFFERENCES IN EDUCATIONAL ACHIEVEMENT

Until 1980s the underachievement of girls was the major concern. However since 1990s girls started to outperform boys in all areas of the education system.

At GCSE girls tend to do better in the majority of subjects:

- 63.4% of girls and 53.8% of boys achieved 5+ A*-C GCSEs or equivalent in 2006 – a gender gap of 9.6%
- largest gender differences (a female advantage of more than 10% on those gaining an A*-C GCSE) are for the Humanities, the Arts and Languages
- smaller gender differences (a female advantage of 5% or less) tend to be in Science and Maths subjects
- girls are more likely than boys to gain an A* grade at GCSE
- boys are a little more likely to gain a G grade at GCSE or to gain no GCSEs at all

At A –Level gender differences in pass rate are much narrower but gender differences still remain:

- across all subjects, the range of difference is 4%. This is in the context of a very high pass rate
- girls perform better than boys in terms of those attaining an A grade (for the majority of subjects), which is a significant change over the last ten years

NOTE: Gender is not the strongest predictor of attainment:

- social class attainment gap at Key Stage 4 (as measured by percentage point difference in attainment between those eligible and not eligible for free school meals) is three times as wide as the gender gap
- some minority ethnic groups attain significantly below the national average and their under-achievement is much greater than the gap between boys and girls

Why are girls doing better than boys?

Mitos and Browne (1998) found

1. the women's movement and feminism raised girls' expectations and self-esteem
2. the increasing number of employment opportunities for women
3. many girls' mother are in paid employment and act as positive role models for them
4. girls' priorities have changed: Sue Sharpe (1976) 'Just Like a Girl'
5. girls are better motivated and organised than boys
6. girls at 16 are seen to be more mature than boys
7. girls benefitted from introduction of coursework in GCSEs/A-Levels
8. national curriculum made more subjects compulsory
9. teachers less likely to gender stereotype girls into set roles or careers

Why do boys underachieve?

1. boys are generally more disruptive in class than girls
2. boys appear to gain 'street cred' by not working hard
3. decline in traditional male jobs
4. teachers tend to have lower expectations of boys
5. lack of male role models in schools
6. laddish subcultures
7. identity crisis in men – uncertain future removes purpose in achieving

8. boys do not like reading as it has become feminised
9. boys tend to overestimate their ability
10. feminisation of assessment – coursework rather than competitive exams

Teacher-pupil interaction affecting the gender gap?

1. Michael Barber (1996) found boys tend to over-estimate their ability, with GCSE results showing the opposite to be true
2. Michelle Stanworth (1983) found boys dominated classroom interaction, pushing girls to the margins which lowered their self-confidence and made them feel less valued, hence girls underestimating their ability
3. Dale Spender (1982) found teachers gave priority to boys giving the impression what girls said was less important
4. Howe (1997) identified the different ways teachers interact with boys and girls - such differences in interaction emerge very early, even in preschool.

Masculine identity can be seen as incompatible with academic success

1. **Forde** (2006) boys are more likely to be influenced by their male peer group which might devalue schoolwork and so put them at odds with academic achievement. It is argued that girls do not experience a conflict of loyalties between friends and school to the same extent as boys
2. **Jackson** 2002 found disruptive behaviour will have a number of benefits by increasing a boy's status with his peer group and can it can deflect attention away from academic performance
3. **Kelly** (1987) found science and the science classroom remain 'masculine' environments with boys dominating science classrooms

Are Changes in the Examination System Responsible for the Gender Gap?

1. Stobart (1992) found a direct relationship between the relative improvement of girls' achievement and the weighting and type of coursework required in different subjects
2. Perceptions of girls' perceived advantage in coursework is high amongst teachers. Over half (53%) of teachers felt that that there was a difference between boys' and girls' ability to do coursework Bishop (1996)

Effects of gender socialization

1. **Lobban** (1974) found evidence of gender stereotyping in children's books with women occupying traditional roles. Best (1993) found little had changed in almost 20 years

2. **Kelly** (1987) – gender stereotyping in science classrooms as well as science text books where women are largely invisible

Continues...

Changes in society

1. Beck (1992) argues in the risk society the rise of individualism allows women to become more self-reliant and self-sufficient through education

ETHNICITY AND ACHIEVEMENT IN SCHOOL

The achievement of ethnic minority pupils in British schools is very complex but the Swann Report of 1985 examined the underachievement of some ethnic minority groups. It is important not to see ethnic minorities as a homogenized (single) group. This is because the patterns of achievement are varied.

Pupils of Indian and Chinese origin tend to do very well, out-performing both the average and the scores of white pupils. By contrast, pupils of Pakistani origin show a very varied pattern of achievement with some doing very well and others relatively poorly. Nevertheless minority ethnic groups tend to underachieve when compared to other population groups.

Your revision will be made easier by using the same approach as used above. Remember to isolate **factors inside school** from those **factors outside school**. Similarly refer back to the previous sections on social-class backgrounds; speech and language codes as well as material and cultural factors.

First some facts (Runnymede Trust, June 2012) which highlight the wide variation across ethnic minority groups:

- Attainment – GCSES (5 A*-C grades including Maths and English) Attainment by ethnicity has improved since 2006/7, and achievement gaps between some ethnic groups and the national level have disappeared. Other ethnic groups, such as Chinese students, have far higher levels of attainment compared to the national level. It is worth highlighting however that Pakistani and Black Caribbean young people still have lower attainment levels than the national level. The data for 2010/11 is as follows:

1. The national level, and the percentage of White British pupils achieving 5 A*-C grades including Maths and English, is 58%. This compares to around 45% in 2006/07

2. Chinese students are the highest attaining group, with 78.5% achieving 5 A*-C grades including Maths and English. This compares to 70% in 2006/07

3. Indian students are the second highest attaining group, with 74.4% achieving 5 A*-C grades including Maths and English. This compares to around 62% in 2006/07

4. Bangladeshi pupils now have a slightly higher attainment rate than White pupils, with 59.7% 5 A*-C grades including Maths and English. This is a massive improvement given that only around 40% achieved this 2006/07, which was 5% less than White pupils and the National Level

5. There has also been an improvement for Black African pupils, with 57.9% achieving 5 A*-C grades including Maths and English, compared to just over 40% achieving this in 2006/07. A similar level of improvement can be seen for mixed White and Black African pupils

6. However, Pakistani and Black Caribbean young people still have lower attainment levels compared to the national level, with 52.6% and 48.6% respectively achieving 5 A*-C grades including Maths and English. This has, however, improved from around 35% for Pakistani and 34% for Black Caribbean pupils in 2006/07

7. Travellers, Gypsies and Roma are still the lowest achieving groups, with 17.5% of Irish Travellers and 10.8% of those from Gypsy or Roma backgrounds achieving 5 A*-C grades including Maths and English. This has improved from 2006/07 when only 5% of these groups combined achieved the required grades.

Factors Outside School

- Social class and material factors – African-Caribbean and Bangladeshi Asians are more likely to be working-class and in poverty and so have a general material disadvantage while Indian and African Asian children are more likely to come from professional/business middle-class backgrounds and the subsequent advantages

- Language – In some ethnic minority households English is not the main language which might cause problems in doing some school work/communication with teachers – but the Swann Report (1985) found language factors were of little importance for the majority as did Modood (1997) who found the high attainment of Indian pupils suggested a second language was not a barrier to achievement

- Racism outside school – Stuart Hall identified a 'culture of resistance' among African-Caribbean youths as a reaction to racial prejudice in society

- Family life – some minority ethnic groups have stronger parental support than others. African-Caribbean have high levels of lone-parenthood and the subsequent material problems. Tony Sewell (1997) argued African-Caribbean boys growing up in lone parent households lacked male role models found in father figure. In contrast Asian family families tend to be extended families offering high levels of support. In addition Archer (2006) found Chinese students and parents put a high value on education as it gave the family a high standing in their community.

Factors Inside School

- Ethnocentric curriculum - school curriculum and the hidden curriculum is too focused on white British culture and adds to the low self-esteem and underachievement of ethnic minorities.

- Racism inside school - The Swann Report found only a small number of teachers were consciously racist. But - Wright (1992) found teachers treated ethnic minority children differently to White children and Gillborn (1990) found African-Caribbean students were more likely to be criticised compared to other ethnic groups committing the same offence – could this lead to Hargreaves self-fulfilling prophecy or Stuart Hall's culture of resistance? Browne (2008) argues negative labelling does not necessarily lead to the negative effects of the self-fulfilling prophecy – see Fuller page 24.

- Setting and streaming - evidence suggests that Black pupils are more likely to be entered for lower tier exams, meaning that these students are only able to able to achieve a maximum grade of a C grade. Stephen J. Ball (2008) has found that Black Caribbean and African students are less likely to be identified for gifted and talented programmes. In contrast, evidence also suggests that Chinese and Indian students are more likely to be entered into higher sets

- Exclusions and discipline - research by David Gillborn and David Drew (2010) found that excluded pupils are 4 times more likely to finish their education without having gained academic qualification. Research by the former Department for Education and Skills (Getting it, Getting it Right 2006) suggest a number of reasons as to why Black pupils are disproportionately excluded, including institutional racism. The same report also found Black pupils encounter both conscious and unconscious prejudice from teachers (both in terms of frequency and severity).

2 **EDUCATION** - MULTIPLE CHOICE QUESTIONS

Q1 The 1944 Education Act established 3 types of schools. This system was known as:

A – the triple system

B- marketization system

C – the tripartite system

D – the post-war system

Q2 The 1944 Education Act established particular types of schools:

A – public schools; fee-paying schools and independent schools

B – Free Schools; Academy Schools and Specialist Schools

C – state schools; comprehensive and Grammar Schools

D – secondary modern schools; secondary technical schools; Grammar Schools

Q3 Comprehensive schools are school which have:

A – no selection test

B – a selection test

C – the 11+ test

D – selection based on parental income

Q4 Comprehensive schools were introduced in order to:

A - reduce social class divisions and break-down social-class barriers

B – increase class divisions and construct social-class barriers

C – reduce social class barriers and introduce marketization of education

D – increase social class barriers and eliminate the marketization of education

Q5 - The 1988 Education Reform Act introduced:

A - competition between schools and turned parents into 'consumers' of education

B – competition between fee-paying schools and turned parents into 'consumers' of education

C – the post-code lottery so schools would compete with each other

D – removed the post-code lottery so schools would no longer compete with each other

Q6 – The 1988 Education Act introduced several educational polices. Three of these are:

A - Comprehensive schools: Ofsted and open enrolment and parental choice

B - Grammar Schools; secondary modern schools and the tripartite system

C - National Curriculum; Ofsted: open enrolment and parental choice

D - secondary modern schools; secondary technical schools; Grammar Schools

Q7 – Writing over 100 years' ago Durkheim argued the main function of education was to bind members of society together. Therefore the education system is:

A – a social adhesive

B - a dysfunctional perquisite

C - a function of society

D – a functional perquisite

Q8 For functionalists one of the key functions of the education system is:

A – to cultivate ascribed status

B – to cultivate achieved status

C – to nurture primary socialization

D – to prevent meritocracy

Q9 - Althusser (Marxist) argued that the main role of education in a capitalist society was the reproduction of:

A - an anti-meritocratic ideology

B – anti-school subcultures

C – an efficient and obedient work force

D – an inefficient and disobedient work force

Q10 – Bowles and Gintis (Marxists) came up with the concept of 'the correspondence principle'. The correspondence principle recognizes:

A - a school's processes are very dissimilar to offices and factories

B - schools legitimate the myth that everyone has an equal chance

C - school processes recognize the myth of meritocracy

D - a school's processes are very similar to those found in offices and factories

Q11 Both functionalist and Marxist perspectives have similarities. They both:

A - tend to ignore social processes within school – except Willis

B - tend to ignore social processes outside school – except Willis

C - tend to ignore social processes in and outside school – except Willis

D - tend to ignore social processes within school – except Willis

Q12 – Which term does Bourdieu use to describe the cultural characteristics and values of each social class?

A – deviancy amplification

B – habitus

C- myth of meritocracy

D - counter-culture

Q13 – Cultural capital as identified by Bourdieu refers to:

A – pupil premium

B – deferred gratification

C – the knowledge, language and values which readily translate into educational capital

D – present time orientation

Q14 – Cultural differences are extended further by examining sub-cultural differences between social groups. Sugarman and Hyman highlighted the effects of socialization because:

A – the middle classes socialized their children to have present time orientation and deferred gratification

B - the middle classes socialized their children to have future time orientation and immediate gratification

C - the middle classes socialized their children to have present time orientation and immediate gratification

D - the middle classes socialized their children to have future time orientation and deferred gratification

Q15 – Bernstein's research focused on linguistic deprivation and is influence on educational success. Bernstein distinguished between:

A – academic speeches codes and non-academic speech codes

B – educational speech codes and vocational speech codes

C – restricted speech codes and elaborated speech codes

D – compensatory speech codes and pupil premium speech codes

Q16 – Pupil premium is used by the state as a form of:

A – compensatory education

B – fatalism

C – homework policy

D – streaming

Q17 - Rutter places great emphasis on the way a school organizes itself. The better their organizational structures and polices the better the school. Three of these policies are:

A – streaming; setting and assemblies

B- setting; homework policy; and sports day

C - marking policy; teacher reward systems; mixed ability classes

D – mixed ability classes; Maths lessons; English lessons

Q18 – Bowles and Ginitis talk of the myth of meritocracy. The myth of meritocracy refers to:

A – schools make sure all students are aware only a select number of people will ever succeed

B – schools tell students failure is a myth

C - schools legitimate the myth that everyone has an equal chance

D – schools tell children if you work hard your dreams will come true

Q19 – The difference between setting and streaming is:

A - setting is where pupils of <u>similar</u> ability are put in different sets (groups) in <u>specific</u> subjects studied, while streaming involves grouping students of <u>similar</u> ability for <u>every</u> subject studied

B – setting is where pupils of <u>different</u> ability are put in different groups/sets in <u>some</u> subjects studied, while streaming involves grouping students of <u>similar</u> ability for <u>every</u> subject studied

C - setting is where pupils of <u>similar</u> ability are put in different groups/sets in specific subjects studied, while streaming involves grouping students of <u>different</u> ability for <u>every</u> subject studied

D - setting is where pupils of different ability are put in different groups/sets in <u>some</u> subjects studied, while streaming involves grouping students of <u>similar</u> ability for <u>some</u> subject studied

Q20 – The halo effect is positive stereotype given by teachers to pupils who:

A – are seen as lazy and troublesome

B – have a 'culture of resistance' to school life

C – are enthusiastic and hardworking

D - form anti-school subcultures

Q21 - Rosenthal and Jacobson's (1968) research found positive and negative labels helped produce:

A – mixed ability classes

B – self-fulfilling prophecy in the classroom

C – material deprivation

D – setting and streaming

Q22 - Mac an Ghaill (1994) identified 3 working-class male subcultures:

A – macho lads; macho lasses; macho people

B – bright lads; average lads; slow lads

C – academic achievers; average achievers; low achievers

D - macho lads; academic achievers; new enterprisers

Q23 – As well as Paul Willis, Colin Lacey's (1970) study of Hightown Grammar school also showed how streaming can lead to the creation of:

A – halo effect

B – anti-school subculture

C – meritocracy

D – cultural capital

Q24 - C. Jackson (2006) 'Lads and Ladettes in School: Gender and the Fear of Failure' looked at how girls are forming anti-school subcultures and becoming:

A – ladettes because of the fear of boys

B – ladettes because of the fear of academic success

C – ladettes because of the fear of academic failure

D - ladettes because of the fear of PE

Q25 – Complete the sentence: 'Gender is not the strongest predictor of attainment…..'

A – because social class attainment gap at Key Stage 4 is three times as wide as the gender gap and some minority ethnic groups achievement is much greater than the gap between boys and girls.

B – because social class attainment gap at Key Stage 4 is insignificant but some minority ethnic groups achievement is much greater than the gap between boys and girls.

C - because social class attainment gap at Key Stage 4 is three times as wide as the gender gap and some minority ethnic groups achievement is insignificant compared to the gap between boys and girls.

D - because social class attainment gap and some minority ethnic groups achievement is the same as than the gap between boys and girls.

Q26 - Teacher-pupil interaction affecting the gender gap. Howe (1997) identified the different ways teachers interact with boys and girls - such differences in interaction emerge….

A – late, around Key Stage 4

B – very late, around Key Stage 5

C - very early, even in preschool

D – early, even in Key Stage 2

Q27 - Masculine identity can be seen as incompatible with academic success. Kelly (1987) found science and the science classroom remain:

A – gender neutral environments with either gender of teacher dominating science classrooms

B – gender neutral environments with nobody dominating science classrooms

C – 'feminine' environments with girls dominating science classrooms

D - 'masculine' environments with boys dominating science classrooms

Q28 – The term ethnocentric curriculum refers to:

A – the school curriculum and the hidden curriculum is too focused on white British culture and adds to the low self-esteem and underachievement of ethnic minorities

B – the school curriculum and the hidden curriculum is not focused enough on white British culture and adds to the low self-esteem and underachievement of ethnic minorities

C – the hidden curriculum is too focused on white British culture and adds to the low self-esteem and underachievement of ethnic minorities

D - school curriculum is too focused on white British culture and adds to the low self-esteem and underachievement of ethnic minorities

Q29 – Family life outside school can affect achievement inside school. Some minority ethnic groups have stronger parental support than others. Chinese students are seen to have high levels of achievement in school because:

A – Archer (2006) found Chinese students and parents put a high value on education as it gave the family a high standing in their community

B- Archer (2006) found Chinese students and parents put a low value on education as it gave the family a high standing in their community

C - Archer (2006) found Chinese students and parents were indifferent to education as it gave the family a high standing in their community

D - Archer (2006) found Chinese students and parents put a high value on education as it gave the family a no standing in their community

Q30 - Ethnicity and achievement. Identify which of the four statements are correct:

A - Stephen J. Ball (2008) found that Black Caribbean and African students are more likely to be identified for gifted and talented programmes. In contrast, evidence also suggests that Chinese and Indian students are less likely to be entered into higher sets

B - Stephen J. Ball (2008) found that Black Caribbean and African students are less likely to be identified for gifted and talented programmes. Evidence also suggests that Chinese and Indian students are also likely to be entered into lower sets

Continues overleaf

C - Stephen J. Ball (2008) found that Black Caribbean and African students are more likely to be identified for gifted and talented programmes. In addition, evidence also suggests that Chinese and Indian students are more likely to be entered into higher sets

D - Stephen J. Ball (2008) found that Black Caribbean and African students are less likely to be identified for gifted and talented programmes. In contrast, evidence also suggests that Chinese and Indian students are more likely to be entered into higher sets

Q31 – Ethnicity and achievement. Identify which of the four statements is correct:

A - African-Caribbean and Bangladeshi Asians are less likely to be working-class and not in poverty and so have a general material advantage while Indian and African Asian children are more likely to come from professional/business middle-class backgrounds and the subsequent advantages

B - African-Caribbean and Bangladeshi Asians are more likely to be working-class and in poverty and so have a general material disadvantage while Indian and African Asian children are more likely to come from professional/business middle-class backgrounds and the subsequent advantages

C - African-Caribbean and Bangladeshi Asians are more likely to be working-class as are Indian and African Asian children and have a general material disadvantage

D - African-Caribbean and Bangladeshi Asians and Indian and African Asian children are more likely to come from professional/business middle-class backgrounds and the subsequent material advantages

Q32 Ethnicity and attainment. Identify which of the three statements is correct:

A - some ethnic groups, such as Chinese students, have far higher levels of attainment compared to the national level

B – some ethnic groups, such as Chinese students, have far lower levels of attainment compared to the national level

C – some ethnic groups, such as Chinese students, have average levels of attainment compared to the national level

Q33 – Ethnicity and attainment. Identify which of the three statements is correct:

A - Chinese students are the highest attaining group, with 95.5% achieving 5 A*-C grades including Maths and English. This compares to 70% in 2006/07

B - Chinese students are the lowest attaining group, with 38.5% achieving 5 A*-C grades including Maths and English. This compares to 70% in 2006/07

C - Chinese students are the highest attaining group, with 78.5% achieving 5 A*-C grades including Maths and English. This compares to 70% in 2006/07

Q34 - Ethnicity and attainment. Identify which of the three statements is correct:

A - Bangladeshi pupils now have a slightly lower attainment rate than White pupils, with 59.7% 5 A*-C grades including Maths and English. This is a massive improvement given that only around 40% achieved this 2006/07, which was 5% less than White pupils

B - Bangladeshi pupils now have a slightly higher attainment rate than White pupils, with 99.7% 5 A*-C grades including Maths and English. This is a massive improvement given that only around 40% achieved this 2006/07, which was 5% less than White pupils

C - Bangladeshi pupils now have a slightly higher attainment rate than White pupils, with 59.7% 5 A*-C grades including Maths and English. This is a massive improvement given that only around 40% achieved this 2006/07, which was 5% less than White pupils

Q35 – Ethnicity and attainment. Identify which of the four statements is correct:

A - Travellers, Gypsies and Roma are still the highest achieving groups, with 97.5% of Irish Travellers and 90.8% of those from Gypsy or Roma backgrounds achieving 5 A*-C grades including Maths and English.

B - Travellers, Gypsies and Roma are still the lowest achieving groups, with 17.5% of Irish Travellers and 10.8% of those from Gypsy or Roma backgrounds achieving 5 A*-C grades including Maths and English.

C - Travellers, Gypsies and Roma are still the average achieving groups, with 47.5% of Irish Travellers and 50.8% of those from Gypsy or Roma backgrounds achieving 5 A*-C grades including Maths and English.

3 **EDUCATION** - MULTIPLE CHOICE ANSWERS

Q1 The 1944 Education Act established 3 types of schools. This system was known as:

C – the tripartite system

Q2 The 1944 Education Act established particular types of schools:

D – secondary modern schools; secondary technical schools; grammar schools

Q3 Comprehensive schools are schools which have:

A – no selection test

Q4 Comprehensive schools were introduced in order to

 A - reduce social class divisions and break-down social-class barriers

Q5 - The 1988 Education Reform Act introduced

A - competition between schools turning parents into 'consumers' of education

Q6 – The 1988 Education Act introduced several educational polices. Three of these are:

C - National Curriculum; Ofsted: open enrolment and parental choice

Q7 – Writing over 100 years' ago Durkheim argued the main function of education was to bind members of society together. Therefore the education system is

D – a functional perquisite

Q8 For functionalists one of the key functions of the education system is

B – to cultivate achieved status

Q9 - Althusser (Marxist) argued that the main role of education in a capitalist society was the reproduction of

C – an efficient and obedient work force

Q10 – Bowles and Gintis (Marxists) came up with the concept of 'the correspondence principle'. The correspondence principle recognizes

D - a school's processes as being very similar to those found in offices and factories

Q11 Both functionalist and Marxist perspectives have similarities. They both

A - tend to ignore social processes within school – except Willis

Q12 – Which term does Bourdieu use to describe the cultural characteristics and values of each social class?

B – habitus

Q13 – Cultural capital as identified by Bourdieu refers to:

C – the knowledge, language and values which readily translate into educational capital

Q14 – Cultural differences are extended further by examining sub-cultural differences between social groups. Sugarman and Hyman highlighted the effects of socialization because:

D - the middle classes socialized their children to have future time orientation and deferred gratification

Q15 – Bernstein's research focused on linguistic deprivation and its influence on educational success. Bernstein distinguished between:

C – restricted speech codes and elaborated speech codes

Q16 – Pupil premium is used by the state as a form of:

A – compensatory education

Q17 - Rutter places great emphasis on the way a school organizes itself. The better their organizational structures and polices the better the school. Three of these policies are:

C - marking policy; teacher reward systems; mixed ability classes

Q18 – Bowles and Ginitis talk of the myth of meritocracy. The myth of meritocracy refers to:

C - schools legitimate the myth that everyone has an equal chance

Q19 – The difference between setting and streaming is:

A - setting is where pupils of similar ability are put in different sets (groups) in specific subjects studied, while streaming involves grouping students of similar ability for every subject studied

Q20 – The halo effect is positive stereotype given by teachers to pupils who

C – are enthusiastic and hardworking

Q21 - Rosenthal and Jacobson's (1968) research found positive and negative labels helped produce

B – self-fulfilling prophecy in the classroom

Q22 - Mac an Ghaill (1994) identified 3 working-class male subcultures

D - macho lads; academic achievers; new enterprisers

Q23 – As well as Paul Willis, Colin Lacey's (1970) study of Hightown Grammar school also showed how streaming can lead to the creation of

B – anti-school subculture

Q24 - C. Jackson (2006) 'Lads and Ladettes in School: Gender and the Fear of Failure' looked at how girls are forming anti-school subcultures and becoming

C – ladettes because of the fear of academic failure

Q25 – Complete the sentence: 'Gender is not the strongest predictor of attainment…..'

A – because social class attainment gap at Key Stage 4 is three times as wide as the gender gap and some minority ethnic groups achievement is much greater than the gap between boys and girls.

Q26 - Teacher-pupil interaction affecting the gender gap. Howe (1997) identified the different ways teachers interact with boys and girls - such differences in interaction emerge….

C - very early, even in preschool

Q27 - Masculine identity can be seen as incompatible with academic success. Kelly (1987) found science and the science classroom remain

D - 'masculine' environments with boys dominating science classrooms

Q28 – The term ethnocentric curriculum refers to

A – the school curriculum and the hidden curriculum is too focused on white British culture and adds to the low self-esteem and underachievement of ethnic minorities

Q29 – Family life outside school can affect achievement inside school. Some minority ethnic groups have stronger parental support than others. Chinese students are seen to have high levels of achievement in school because

A – Archer (2006) found Chinese students and parents put a high value on education as it gave the family a high standing in their community

Q30 - Ethnicity and achievement. Highlight which of the following four statements is correct:

D - Stephen J. Ball (2008) found that Black Caribbean and African students are less likely to be identified for gifted and talented programmes. In contrast, evidence also suggests that Chinese and Indian students are more likely to be entered into higher sets

Q31 – Ethnicity and achievement. Highlight which of the following three statements is correct:

B - African-Caribbean and Bangladeshi Asians are more likely to be working-class and in poverty and so have a general material disadvantage while Indian and African Asian children are more likely to come from professional/business middle-class backgrounds and the subsequent advantages

Q32 Ethnicity and attainment. Identify which of the three statements is correct.

A - some ethnic groups, such as Chinese students, have far higher levels of attainment compared to the national level

Q33 – Ethnicity and attainment. Identify which of the three statements is correct.

C - Chinese students are the highest attaining group, with 78.5% achieving 5 A*-C grades including Maths and English. This compares to 70% in 2006/07

Q34 - Ethnicity and attainment. Identify which of the three statements is correct:

C - Bangladeshi pupils now have a slightly higher attainment rate than White pupils, with 59.7% 5 A*-C grades including Maths and English. This is a massive improvement given that only around 40% achieved this 2006/07, which was 5% less than White pupils

Q35 – Ethnicity and attainment. Identify which of the three statements is correct:

B - Travellers, Gypsies and Roma are still the lowest achieving groups, with 17.5% of Irish Travellers and 10.8% of those from Gypsy or Roma backgrounds achieving 5 A*-C grades including Maths and English.

4 **EDUCATION** - SINGLE QUESTIONS

Q1 Identify two reasons why are girls have higher levels of achievement in school than boys

Q2 Identify two reasons why girls have high levels of achievement in school (this question doesn't mention boys)

Q3 Identify two reasons why boys are underachieving in school (this question makes no mention of girls)

Q4 Identify two functions that the education system might perform

Q5 Identify two polices contributing to the marketization of education

Q6 Identify two ways in which cultural deprivation might affect work-class pupil under achievement in school (this question is not asking about material factors)

Q7 Functionalists have their own perspective on the purpose of the education system. Identify two criticisms other sociologists might make of the functionalist perspective.

Q8 Identify three ways in which social policies may have influenced social-class differences in educational achievement

Q9 Identify three factors outside school which may have aided girls' achievement in school (you do not mention factors inside school)

Q10 Identify three factors within schools which may have affect the educational underachievement of some ethnic minority groups.

Q11 – Identify three ways in which Marxists would say the education system and its processes replicate the workplace.

Q12 – Identify three types of school subcultures

Q13 – Identify three reasons why working-class parents might not attend parents' evenings

Q14 - Identify three processes inside school which may have an effect on pupils from different social groups

Q15 - Identify three processes outside school which may have an effect on pupils from different social groups

Q16 – identify one criticism of labelling theory

Q17 – Identify three ways in which a school's curriculum might be ethnocentric

Q18 – Identify two policies designed to encourage the introduction of market forces in the education system

Q19 – Identify two ways in which pupils identities might be shaped by their experiences at school

5 **EDUCATION** - SINGLE QUESTIONS: THE ANSWERS

Q1 Identify two reasons why are girls have higher levels of achievement in school than boys

- the women's movement and feminism raised girls' expectations and self-esteem
- the increasing number of employment opportunities for women
- many girls' mother are in paid employment and act as positive role models for them
- girls' priorities have changed: Sue Sharpe (1976) 'Just Like a Girl'
- girls are better motivated and organised than boys
- girls at 16 are seen to be more mature than boys
- girls benefitted from introduction of coursework in GCSEs/A-Levels
- national curriculum made more subjects compulsory
- teachers less likely to gender stereotype girls into set roles or careers

Q2 Identify two reasons why girls have high levels of achievement in school (this question doesn't mention boys)

- the women's movement and feminism raised girls' expectations and self-esteem
- the increasing number of employment opportunities for women
- many girls' mother are in paid employment and act as positive role models for them
- girls' priorities have changed: Sue Sharpe (1976) 'Just Like a Girl'

Q3 Identify two reasons why boys are underachieving in school (this question makes no mention of girls)

- boys are generally more disruptive in class than girls
- boys appear to gain 'street cred' by not working hard
- decline in traditional male jobs
- teachers tend to have lower expectations of boys
- lack of male role models in schools
- laddish subcultures
- identity crisis in men – uncertain future removes purpose in achieving
- boys do not like reading as it has become feminised
- boys tend to overestimate their ability
- feminisation of assessment – coursework rather than competitive exams

Q4 Identify two functions that the education system might perform

- secondary socialization
- gender role socialization
- division of labour
- role allocation
- establishment of universalistic values
- meritocracy
- value consensus through the hidden curriculum
- meritocracy
- competition

Q5 Identify two polices contributing to the marketization of education

- publication of school league tables showing exam results
- schools competing for pupils
- publication of Ofsted reports
- schools opting out of local authority control
- encouragement of different types of schools - Free Schools; Academies etc
- 1988 Education Reform Act

Q6 Identify two ways in which cultural deprivation might affect work-class pupil under achievement in school (this question is not asking about material factors)

- immediate gratification
- present time orientation
- lack of cultural capital
- parental attitudes to education
- sense of fatalism
- speech and language codes
- parents level of educational achievement

Q7 Functionalists have their own perspective on the purpose of the education system. Identify two criticisms other sociologists might make of the functionalist perspective.

- Marxists point out meritocracy is a myth
- Marxists would point out to functionalists how the role allocation of jobs is not conducted via meritocracy as many jobs are allocated via social-class background
- Marxists would point out to functionalists how the education system does not encourage the sharing of values through consensual processes rather the education system is there to promote a ruling-class ideology
- Paul Willis' would point out how a number of pupils reject the values being taught via the educations system. Instead of passively accepting what is being delivered/communicated they reject it and can form anti-school subcultures
- Feminists would point out the school system encourages gender role allocation eg too few girls choose to study engineering
- Feminists would point out the school system encourages patriarchal gender regimes e.g. many school leadership teams are male dominated

Q8 Identify three ways in which social policies may have influenced social-class differences in educational achievement

- Parental power as consumers of education – sometimes known as parentocracy
- New vocationalism
- Free school meals
- Compensatory education policies
- Correspondence principle
- Expansion of Higher Education
- Marketization
- Private schooling

Q9 Identify three factors outside school which may have aided girls' achievement in school (you do not mention factors inside school)

- Women in paid employment
- Feminism
- Parental encouragement
- Equal opportunities in the workplace – career and pay
- Changing nature of work – more feminized jobs
- Changing patterns of work – more flexible shift work allowing women to balance child-care with paid work
- Increase in divorce rates
- Increase in lone parenting
- Changing girls aspirations
- Different leisure patterns – girls prefer reading/conversation improving their linguistic skills needed for literature based subjects. Much of this comes from be socialized by their mothers reading to them as children

Q10 Identify three factors within schools which may have affect the educational underachievement of some ethnic minority groups.

- self-fulfilling prophecy from teacher labelling
- teacher's negativity
- teacher racism
- ethnocentric curriculum
- discriminatory admission and selection processes
- institutional racism
- anti-school subcultures
- culture of resistance – Hall

Q11 – Identify three ways in which Marxists would say the education system and its processes replicate the workplace.

- Hierarchy of authority
- Correspondence principle
- Both driven by competitive processes
- Class alienation – working class feel alienated in a predominantly middle-class institution
- Status difference – wealthy children go to fee-paying schools (end up having high-flying careers)) while the majority attend state schools (end up having jobs with limited opportunities)
- Reward systems – schools reward good work with 'stars' & 'merits' which is replicated in work-place to relieve the monotony
- Fragmented timetable learning – work – break-time – back to work – break-time – back to work

Q12 – Identify three types of school subcultures

- Male anti-school subcultures
- Female school subcultures
- African-Caribbean male subcultures
- African-Caribbean female subcultures

Q13 – Identify three reasons why working-class parents might not attend parents' evenings

- Lack of interest
- Feeling of inferiority against predominantly middle-class teachers
- More likely to be on shift-work than middle-class parents
- Having to work longer hours to compensate for low pay
- Can't afford child-minder in order to attend
- Lack of education themselves so unable to understand subject based targets set by the teacher

Q14 - Identify three processes inside school which may have an effect on pupils from different social groups

- Labelling
- Halo effect
- Self-fulfilling prophecy
- Ethnocentric curriculum
- Setting/streaming
- Mixed ability classes
- Subcultures
- School organization
- Gender regimes
- Open enrolment

Q15 - Identify three processes outside school which may have an effect on pupils from different social groups

- Material deprivation
- Cultural deprivation
- Speech codes
- Parental interest
- Parental education
- Parental occupation
- Cultural capital – habitus
- Compensatory education
- Marketization – choosing school via income – postcode lottery

Q16 – identify one criticism of labelling theory

- Too deterministic – some pupils remove the labels through hard work
- Ignores other influences – eg material deprivation
- Doesn't consider the influence of wider society in the construction of labels given out in classroom eg race
- Assumes pupils are aware they have been labelled – some aren't
- Assumes there's always a self-fulfilling prophecy – some pupils ignore the label

Q17 – Identify three ways in which a school's curriculum might be ethnocentric

- Not providing Halal meals
- History lesson too focused on White history
- School holidays constructed around Christian calendar
- Religious assemblies delivered from a singular religious perspective
- Uniform and dress codes designed around Western values
- Dress/changing rooms for PE and Games lessons structured around Western values

Q18 – Identify two policies designed to encourage the introduction of market forces in the education system

- The National Curriculum
- National testing (SATS)
- National league tables
- Open enrolment and parental choice
- Ofsted
- Local management of schools
- Schools having control of their own admissions criteria
- Schools having their own discipline and exclusion criteria

Q19 – Identify two ways in which pupils identities might be shaped by their experiences at school

- Subject choice – though national curriculum aimed to limit differences between gender regimes in subject choice physics, chemistry and Maths are still seen as male subjects while art, English and dance are seen as girl subjects
- Gender socialization – gender stereotypes were still found in many school books (page 27)
- Gender socialization - masculine identity can be seen as incompatible with academic success (27)
- Pupil subcultures (pages 24 & 25)
- Teacher-pupil interaction affecting the gender gap (page 27)
- Differing rates of achievement – girls outperforming boys due to wider social changes (page 26)
- feminisation of assessment – coursework rather than competitive exams
- gendered language – (page 21)
- women in the curriculum (page 21)

6 GLOSSARY

Anthropology – studying the societies and cultures, especially those of pre-industrial societies found around the globe

Bourgeoisie – a term from Marxism denoting a social-class composed of people whose livelihood comes from the ownership of capital

Capitalism – an economy based on the production of goods for sale (commodities) using waged labour; capitalists own the means of production in order to make profit.

Culture – the beliefs, values and customs of a society or social group

Ethnicity – the members of a social group who share common characteristics such as religion, language or race

Ethnography – a research method based on the detailed observation of a culture or group

Experiment/laboratory experiment –a research procedure which attempts to test a hypothesis by manipulating aspects of reality to see whether the outcome suggested by the hypothesis occurs.

Ideology – a system of ideas and beliefs which may reflect the interests of a particular social group

Institutional racism – discrimination against a particular ethnic or racial groups which is built on the processes, procedures and policies of an institution whether or not the discrimination is intended

Marketization of education - where parents have the power and choice to make a decision and "shop around" as consumers of education to see which is the best school to send their child to

Net-migration - The rate of people moving into a country less the number of people moving out of the same country

Patriarchy – a social system of male dominance based on assumptions of male superiority

Power – the capacity of individuals, groups, or social-classes to achieve goals and protect interests

Proletariat – a term from Marxism denoting a social-class of people whose livelihood comes from selling their labour in exchange for wages (see bourgeoisie)

Racism – belief that biologically rooted characteristics determine social activities and abilities as well as the inherent superiority and inferiority of different races

Self-fulfilling prophecy – happens when people act in response to behaviour which has been predicted of them which subsequently makes the prediction come true

Social class – classifications of people with broadly similar occupations, resources or styles of living

Social policy - are public services that aid the well-being of citizens

Society – the total entity formed by individuals and groups and their social relations most commonly located within a nation state

Stereotyping – where generalized qualities or attributes of a social group often prejudice the representation of that group

State – a set of institutions and system of government which exercises control over a specific geographical area and the population of that area.

Underclass – a concept used to characterize those occupying the lowest positions in society

Vocational education - educational training that provides practical experience in a particular occupational field such as learning a trade

Welfare state – the social and political institutions by which the state assumes a responsibility for the health and social welfare of its citizens

7 INDEX

ABOUT THE AUTHOR

The contents of the book have been written by sociologytwynham.com. For any other information or question you would like answering please contact us via the website. For other information on books in the series please visit the Revision page at sociologytwynham.com.